Middle-Class JOBS

Policies to Create Millions

FIRST EDITION

MARK BARTOLD

Fulton Books, Inc.
Meadville, PA

Published by Fulton Books 2022

ISBN 978-1-63985-734-0 (paperback)
ISBN 978-1-63985-735-7 (digital)

Printed in the United States of America

To all the hardworking families in the United States and the world

To the mothers and fathers working hard to pay the
bills so their children can have a roof over their head,
clothes on their backs, and food on the table

CONTENTS

PREFACE

I started to write this book back in October 2008. The country was in an economic crash: Goldman Sachs competitors were being wiped out. Banks were getting the houses back. Job losses were increasing every week. Gas prices were $4 and up depending where you lived.

I sent fifty copies of rough drafts to politicians all over the country. Every Christmas, I would get a Christmas card from the vice presidential mansion because I sent a book to Mrs. Joe Biden.

I decided to rewrite and publish this book because the economy for the middle-class families is still struggling with the added burdens of more college debt because of the necessity of college degrees in the workforce.

I broke the chapters into policies because in order to get money for job creation, you have to have policies to present to lawmakers for the bills to be made and voted on. I listed examples of middle-class jobs that can be created in each chapter, and there are some overlaps in jobs across multiple policies, which is kind of good to be able to cover multiple areas of need in this country with jobs.

The jobs that I will list at the end of each policy would have a minimum pay of $15 an hour. With higher-paying jobs in the mix and costs involved in training and uniforms, I have used an "$80,000 a year" base cost per job created in these policies. For the obvious higher-paying jobs, there will be a multiplier noted, for example: two times cost or three times cost for doctors, judges, upper management, and other monetary considerations.

Enjoy the read, and you will find that the policies are easy to modify up or down in size to fit whatever budgets or industry projects that are planned.

New City Development

This is the most extravagant policy, but it is the easiest way to put a million people to work and add an additional million people every five years after that.

The first step is to determine the location for a major city to be built and then determine what kind of city you want to build.

For example, Dubai always fascinated me on how a city full of rich people could be built in such a short time frame. There was a location by the water and in an area that could sustain monstrous skyscrapers. Islands were created in images of palm trees and even a world map of islands to help capture the imagination of the people that would live there, shopping malls, museums, Lamborghinis, indoor ski slopes, and all the comforts of big city living located in the desert.

Since we live in the United States, the new cities would need to have a majority of middle-class people living there with 10 percent rich and less than 10 percent people with special needs. A freshwater source, cropland, solar, and wind would be perfect locations for building a new city and having an energy efficient, zero carbon emission city would be the best way to start our policy example.

Now that we have the goal set, it's time to finally put some people to work. Zoning, water tests, ground tests, architecture of city, as well as the placement of the water purification system, windmills, solar panels, crops, plants, trees, sidewalks, and electric mass transit system will require a coordinated team of planners, architects, industrial engineers, and private industry representatives to establish the size and cost of the new utilities and construction. Planning for efficiency of usage, air quality, and psychological studies would need to be done to consider the right light and colors to use in the city. In addition to living quarters, shops, and restaurants, there will be a need for a city hall, fire department, police, hospital, churches, community centers, schools from K to masters programs and trade schools. Think of it like SimCity-type game but for real.

Now I will list the various living wage jobs that can be created with an example of how many jobs can be created and how much it will cost. How you find or pay for the policy will be discussed in a later chapter.

Living wage of $15 an hour and the costs to implement for a yearly total of eighty thousand per job unit in which some jobs are two or three times multiplier.

Labor breakdown for "New City Development" would take another book and would depend on the size of the project. I will give you a generic two-phased assumption of what it would cost for a million jobs.

Phase 1—planning, designing, logistics and land use studies, and providing access to project by way of land, air, and sea.
40,000 jobs at $80,000 = $3.2 billion
40,000 jobs at $160,000 = $6.4 billion
20,000 jobs at $240,000 = $9.6 billion

Phase 1—total jobs of 100,000, costing $19.2 billion.

Phase 2—construction and support services.
600,000 jobs at $80,000 = $48.0 billion
280,000 jobs at $160,000 = $44.8 billion
20,000 jobs at $240,000 = $4.8 billion

Phase 2—total jobs of 900,000, costing $97.6 billion.

A majority of phase 1 jobs can continue into phase 2 to implement the phase 1 work as well as follow-ups and inspections.

With that being said, any employees that are not needed in phase 2 can be retrained or transferred to other cities across the country.

Immigration

Immigration policy has been discussed for the last few decades and has never satisfied any of the critics no matter what party you are from. Now is the time to fix the immigration system that will last centuries.

World War II as well as other wars produced challenging immigration policies for immigrants to come to the United States, yet we managed to figure out how to organize millions of people to be placed in our nation of immigrants. In the last forty years, immigration has been a political nightmare. Both parties have had policies that have either been detrimental to immigrants or had no policy at all, which led to distrust in the system all together.

Immigration officers will be needed to process more immigrants legally. Fees are paid by most immigrants and work visas shall be offered to the seasonal workers. The worker shortages of low-wage jobs in 2021 was multilayered. Immigrants were demonized between 2017 and 2021, and Central and South America had outbreaks of Covid-19, causing loss of life and lockdowns. Most of the ten to twelve million illegal immigrants either went back to their home countries or went to other countries that were in need of workers. In addition, some may have got sick and died. At the time of my transcribing of this book, over 650,000 people died in the US from Covid-19. Retirement-aged workers who worked passed retirement age decided it was better to retire than to put themselves at risk at work.

Immigrants are needed more than ever to help our country recover and grow. From low-wage workers to doctors and engineers, we need workers.

China has over one billion more people than we do, and with the pressure against China increasing every day, the global economy has been fractured, which has led to jobs opening back up in the US that were exported thirty years ago. The challenge is finding enough workers to fill positions as well as competent trained workers. Lowering the age for workers will no doubt come up, but it would be a mistake to have young workers working when they need to finish trade schools or college first.

It is time to welcome immigrants to the United States again. It is in our best interest, and we need to increase our language to Spanish and English. The increase in Spanish-Americans will exceed any immigrant migration in US history.

A framework of processing facilities and immigrant services will need to be planned. The cities that will house the new immigrants will need funding to offset budgets for schools, social services translators, and workforce development officers. The work visa workers will go to existing locations that farmworkers currently go to. Visa workers for other types of work will need to be verified with more care.

Border security will continue. Every nation should have border security to the levels needed to keep their nations safe. Increased immigration officers to process immigrants before they even get to the borders will help trim down the border crossings. Many immigrants pay smugglers more to cross the border than if they did it legally. Increase in military forces by four million will increase our security and readiness, and immigrants usually are part of our military.

Eighty million immigrants in the next twenty years will require four million new immigrants a year. These new immigrants will add to our workforce, pay taxes, buy houses, buy cars, contribute to the society, and help build our nation into a well-rounded free country.

Immigration officers—20,000 jobs at $80,000 = $1.6 billion.
Work visa officers—20,000 jobs at $80,000 = $1.6 billion.
Border patrol—10,000 jobs at $80,000 = $0.8 billion.
Immigration lawyers—10,000 jobs at $160,000 = $1.6 billion.
Immigration paralegals—20,000 jobs at $80,000 = $1.6 billion.
Judges—1,000 jobs at $240,000 = $0.24 billion.
Police and prison guards—20,000 jobs at $80,000 = $1.6 billion.
Job placement officers—20,000 jobs at $80,000 = $1.6 billion.
Social service workers—50,000 jobs at $80,000 = $4 billion.
Nurses and support staff—50,000 jobs at $160,000 = $8 billion.
Teachers/bilinguals—100,000 jobs at $80,000 = $8 billion.
School support staff—100,000 jobs at $80,000 = $8 billion.
Homeland security / FBI—40,000 jobs at $160,000 = $6.4 billion.
Foreign service workers—50,000 jobs at $160,000 = $8 billion.
Increase armed services—100,000 jobs at $160,000 = $16 billion.
There is total increase in immigration jobs and jobs that provide support for increased immigrant presence.

Grand total jobs—611,000 for $69.04 billion.

I want to take this time to apologize to anyone that may be offended in any way by my occasional political comments when presenting my observations. I have multiple political views that are left, right, center, and unique at times. I am registered, unaffiliated, and have voted for all major party candidates as well as the so-called unwinnable parties. I have only had one candidate whom I wished I had not voted for in a governors' race. Most of my candidates lost, but I can sleep good at night knowing I voted my beliefs.

Now some people say that my one vote caused another candidate to win. I would never presume to believe I have that kind of power. Most democracies have multiple candidates to choose from, and having the top 3 candidates from the major parties and at least one from each minor party would help provide a more transparent general election. The vote against a candidate is not a vote for a candidate; it is a lose, lose philosophy. Lesser of two evils is failing to acknowledge the other party candidates that are running for office.

The other party candidates are assumed to be losers, and then the lesser of the two loser candidates makes it a choice of four or more losers for president.

I regularly say that the elections have been decided in the primaries when nobody votes. In the end, most people wind up with a politician they did not want. A good example is the National Football League (NFL) has thirty-two teams. I am a Giants fan. The thirty-one other teams are those I do not wish to go to the Super Bowl. During the season, most people do not even watch football. The Super Bowl comes, and the Giants are not in the race, so I am indifferent of who wins and may even cheer for a rival team or player on a team. In addition to thirty teams of fans not having their team in the Super Bowl, millions of people watch the game who never watch football. Why? Commercials. If you ask anybody if they like commercials, nobody says yes. Around the Super Bowl, people go, "I love watching the commercials." Elections are in the same way. Most people don't pay attention to politics until the November elections.

Again, I apologize ahead of time, and please remember these policies are just an outline of ideas to put Americans to work and grow the country into a juggernaut that has to compete with the rest of the world.

POLICY 3

Health Care

Basic nurses will be needed on a grand scale because of baby boomers retiring and people living longer than ever before. Large numbers of legal and illegal immigrants coming to this country will require more bilingual nurses, specialty nurses in various diseases that are not common in our part of the world, and nurses for people suffering from war-torn regions and natural disasters.

Terrorism is not going away anytime soon, and having emergency-response nurses qualified to deal with terror attacks from conventional and unconventional means must be considered for the future.

Basic nurses for schools can help with detection of disease, and they can teach safety classes. The school nurse could also be the safety inspector for the school and request safety devices when needed.

Registered nurses are already in short demand and, in some cases, have to travel out of state to treat a patient that doesn't require a doctor's presence. These jobs are crucial because doctor positions are going to be very short with higher-elderly population in this country.

Paramedics and firefighters will also be needed to respond to all the reasons just given. Forest fires, flooding, and other natural disasters are on the rise, so training in these areas is of utmost demand because there usually isn't a second chance to get it right.

Medical research will be continued and expanded to try and conquer the cancers and viruses that continue to plague our society, which will require more nurses to assist the doctors as well as premed doctors. Premed doctors should be tuition-free to individuals who qualify. (More discussion on this subject—tuition—will be covered in the trade school and education policies.) Research will be greatly benefitted by the up-and-coming doctors. The premeds could do the actual studies as they are becoming doctors. For the reasons stated above, doctors will need to be trained in a variety of situations.

The military is another avenue to learn the skills of a doctor and brings all the regular problems that civilians are subjected to as well as potential biochemical, radiation, and other military grade exposure problems.

It takes a long time for a doctor to get certified, so we should help as best as we can to encourage people to become doctors that qualify. Accountability of the doctors' training will limit the future doctors from malpractice suits. Qualifications and accountability are necessities. I have included those philosophies throughout this book and will be discussed in greater detail in the later chapter.

Mental health professionals are needed more than ever to keep up with the rising mental health crisis. Many people are diagnosed with a mental illness but have lived with the illness for years prior to being diagnosed. My mom was shopping at a grocery store, and the cashier had bipolar disorder. The cashier proceeded to explain to my mom that if she needed to talk about her bipolar disorder, she could talk to her. My mom was surprised by her comment and went to the doctor where she was diagnosed for bipolar disorder. How many times have you said "That boy or girl is crazy"? Well, maybe you are right. That being said, what are people supposed to do? All the shootings over the last few decades have discussed the fact that the gun does not kill, it's the person. Nothing is done about military grade weapons; in addition, nothing is done about mental illness.

The health department and social services have been overwhelmed with people needing health services. Social workers could use more help and training to provide the services needed to the underprivileged.

Child safety and food safety are concerns lately because of the food supply coming from third world nations in some cases as well as developing nations. Questions concerning food include: Is the water supply for cleaning the food safe? Are the canning factories clean? Are there food inspectors inspecting the food? In addition, toys made with various chemicals could cause problems for children in short- or long-term health.

Medical science and research will need more scientists and chemists to keep on top of disease control and solving fatal illnesses. Prescription drugs should be monitored for price gouging. Too many people have died because of greed in the pharmaceutical industry.

FEMA needs to be improved drastically to respond to disasters that are getting bigger and more common. A quick medical facility such as a MASH unit could be flown to any location where medical care could be done on victims from a disaster. The patients could be flown in to the MASH unit by a helicopter or brought in by an ambulance. Most of the times, hospitals in such areas either have no power or have been destroyed. Hurricane Katrina, which hit New Orleans and broke the levee, is a good example of future disasters that will need unprecedented response. September 11, 2001 is another reminder of the danger's fires cause in reference to the chemicals inhaled at the terror attack site of the World Trade Center. Many people have died from the chemicals that the responders and recovery personnel were exposed to. A similar example would be the Agent Orange that was sprayed in Vietnam during the Vietnam War, exposing soldiers as well as civilians, which caused sickness and death of thousands of people.

In 1945, there were two cities in Japan destroyed by nukes. Disasters such as the Three Mile Island accident in US, Chernobyl disaster in Russia, and Fukushima Daiichi nuclear disaster in Japan, which happened in 2011, have caused great health risks. It's just a matter of time before another nuclear attack or accident. We need to be more prepared for that eventuality, and it will require well-trained health specialists, scientists, and chemists.

The professors and medical training schools needed for the vast medical field that needs upgrading will be expensive. The clear solution is to get rid of the insurance companies because they complicate the service of the patient by bogging the doctors with paperwork and take a large fee. Lawsuits and deadbeat patients add to the costs. Wall

Street makes billions on the health care industry. Universal health care makes the best sense because all Americans have a social security number and can be signed in to an emergency room or a doctor's office and must be sent an email or letter to that effect so that fraud is limited. For example, let's say a doctor charges for an office visit on a Monday, and the owner of the social security number gets the email and says no, that is not me, then they can try to get whoever is using their social security number. A bill from the doctor stating the office visit without an email or letter can be challenged, and if there are a bunch of cases of that activity at a doctor's office, then there would be an investigation. More about accountability will be discussed in later chapters.

Now I will list the various living wage jobs that can be created with an example of how many jobs can be created and how much it will cost. How you find or pay for the policy will be discussed in a later chapter.

A living wage of $15 an hour and the costs to implement for a yearly total of 80,000 per job unit in which some jobs are two or three times multiplier.

Basic nurses—200,000 jobs at 80,000 = $16 billion.
Registered nurses—100,000 jobs at 160,000 = $16 billion.
Paramedics and firefighters—100,000 jobs at 80,000 = $8 billion.
Social services department—100,000 jobs at $80,000 = $8 billion.
Support staff—100,000 jobs at $80,000 = $8 billion.
Premed doctors—40,000 jobs at $240,000 = $9.6 billion.
Mental health professionals—40,000 jobs at $160,000 = $6.4 billion.
Food and child safety—40,000 jobs at $80,000 = $3.2 billion.
Medical scientists—20,000 jobs at $240,000 = $4.8 billion.
Professors for medicine—20,000 jobs at $240,000 = $4.8 billion.
Medical system committee—20,000 jobs at $240,000 = $4.8 billion.
Disaster relief—20,000 jobs at $80,000 = $1.6 billion.

The grand total is 800,000 jobs for $91.2 billion.

Keep in mind that each job created helps local tax revenue, home sales, car sales, retail sales, and the social rewards that are not expressed in dollars but can be tracked in lower crime, lower domestic violence, lower suicide rates, increased health of population, and increased productivity.

These jobs are above and beyond existing professionals and should not be considered for funding existing programs. The goal is to create jobs and not bait and switch like the lottery system for education does.

You can scale the policy to eighty thousand jobs at $9.12 billion as an example or target certain jobs like just nurses for $16 billion or just mental health professionals for $6.4 billion. The option is yours and depends of the scale of the policy.

A state would have to lower scale and nationally, which I had in mind might have to cover multiple years so don't get to bent up on the billions of dollars. Keep in mind, we spend over $720 billion a year on military and never ask how we pay for it, but keep reading and I will tell you how we pay for it, and how we can create more jobs in the military for less dollars than we pay now later in this book.

POLICY 4

Personal Security

Police officers are essential to our society because they enforce the laws that local, state, and federal governments put into place. Timothy McVeigh, the Oklahoma City bomber, confessed to the bombing when he was pulled over for a routine traffic stop. There are many examples of criminals being caught in this manner. With that being said, many routine stops are for noncriminals and have resulted in harassment, injuries, lawsuits, and even death of citizens as well as police officers.

Police officer trainings are extensive and needs to be modified in areas that have excessive force issues. A precinct-by-precinct retrain in conduct and tactics can be very effective in the reduction of unnecessary violence and would build trust in the communities. With that being said, police officers need to defend themselves, and one of the ways they protect themselves is by using offensive tactics before they are put in a need of being in a defensive position. Sounds complicated, but military and police-minded people know exactly what I am talking about.

Bill Clinton signed a bill that put hundred thousand more police officers on the streets when he was the president. The program expired and was not renewed. The 9/11 caused many more police officers to be transferred to Afghanistan, Iraq, and other locations that were not their duties as police officers. Due to shortages, many officers retired early than to work under stressful situations. This shortage of police officers created a spike in crime. Militarization of the police forces accelerated to provide police with more fire power, combat vehicles, and personnel protective equipment to try to offset shortages of officers. The amount of stress multiplied by the increased number of offenders created a list of priority calls or reaction calls as opposed to standard policing of deterrence.

As the wars in Afghanistan and Iraq started to be reeled in, many police officers returned to work. Many veterans took police training classes and found jobs as state troopers, deputy sheriffs, police officers, and college campus police officers. This influx of combat-ready soldiers hitting the streets of our free and loving nation has created a hyperfocus on police tactics. I wish to thank the officers on the job for the life-and-death decisions they have to make every day when they approach suspects' cars, houses, or on the streets. It is a fine line of being a Miami vice cop, being a Beverly hills cop, or a combat zone police action cop.

Detectives were equally short on demand and repeat-offending crimes would increase due to cases not being solved in a timely matter, if the cases were solved at all. Increasing detectives to make sure cases are opened and closed in a sufficient amount of time will ensure crime is kept in check.

Federal Bureau of Investigation has a crime lab in Washington, DC. The amount of time it takes to test a suspect's lab results in a case could be weeks and especially if the suspect is on west coast or on other side of the planet. Building another FBI lab on the west coast and overseas would cut down time-sensitive cases. In addition to the labs, the FBI needs to be better prepared, if they are not already, analyzing data and information on suspects. Once suspects are on radar, decisions must be made on how to proceed forward without letting the suspects cause another 9/11 or 2021 United States Capitol Attack. Computer hackers, white-collar crimes, interstate criminals, kidnappers, and many other crimes under the FBI need agents to work on them.

There should be active shooter training for police officers, teachers, school staff, and students. Students should also be trained on how to respond to an active shooter.

On the need for additional training of law enforcement, school personnel and students will require more teachers and instructors. Just like the military, training is essential to provide safety for the weapon's user, safety of the partner, and safety of the people you are trying to help. Without proper training, accidents, miscommunication, misconduct, ill will, and unsuccessful job performance is exposed. It is important that the conduct of the trainee be top notch and professional. The recruits need to be knowledgeable of the laws they have sworn to protect. The recruits also need to know how to deal with people and ask the right questions of suspects or witnesses. The instructors will need to be able to teach these skills, and the testing will be written and hands-on training will need to be intensified.

Social services handle an inordinate number of cases, and from time to time, there are tragedies that happen because of overburdened caseloads.

Activity coaches can help teens stay off the streets and mentor good habits over bad habits.

Nurses for schools can provide CPR training, early warning of outbreaks, and provide health advice for cafeterias and health choices to students or parents if asked.

Lifeguards could provide CPR training and swimming lessons.

Food and water safety has been a concern over the years, and the best way to keep everyone safe is to keep up inspections, which will require more and more inspectors as the number of companies grows expediently. China had a problem with their milk supply and had cross-contaminated baby food, chocolates, and other products made from dairy. Other food supply outbreaks include mad cow disease, bird flu, and many others. Water pipes in Flint, Michigan, made news years ago, but many cases across the country do not make the news. Oil pipeline protests usually concern safety of water supplies.

Toy safety years ago had one inspector inspecting all the toys entering the US. I would hope that there are more people inspecting infant products. Safety of our children from lead paint of whatever is no good if other nations can import them for sale while a US company knows not to use lead paint.

Personnel safety is a second amendment right and firearm safety training should be mandatory. Self-defense courses should also be offered to those who wish to spend their time being trained.

Drug addiction has caused a major risk to our personnel security as a nation, and the failure of the war on drugs needs to set new goals because business, as usual, is not working. I will cover the war on drugs segment in the "Homeland Security" chapter. With that being said, the war on drugs covers many segments and having policies chip at the large issue in different ways is a good thing. Counselors, nurses, doctors, law enforcement, and legal issues can be addressed in this type of bill.

Many of the jobs in this section, as well as this book, require skilled labor. To implement the policies at a reduced labor cost, entry-level workers can assist the skilled workers.

Police officers—50,000 jobs at $80,000 = $4 billion.
Social workers—50,000 jobs at $80,000 = $4 billion.
School security—100,000 jobs at $80,000 = $8 billion.
Nurses—100,000 jobs at $80,000 = $8 billion.
Interns—100,000 jobs at $80,000 = $8 billion.
Mental health professionals—25,000 jobs at $160,000 = $4 billion.
Counselors/teachers—20,000 jobs at $160,000 = $3.2 billion.
Prison guards—20,000 jobs at $80,000 = $1.6 billion.
Detectives—20,000 jobs at $160,000 = $3.2 billion.
FBI—20,000 jobs at $160,000 = $3.2 billion.
Paralegals—50,000 jobs at $80,000 = $4 billion.
Lawyers—10,000 jobs at $160,000 = $1.6 billion.
Judges—1,000 jobs at $240,000 = $0.24 billion.

The grand total is 566,000 jobs for $51.44 billion.

POLICY 5

Homeland Security

Homeland Security is a security apparatus that was created after September 11, 2001, attacks on the United States. The purpose of Homeland Security was to coordinate all the intelligence agencies with the police and emergency response organizations into one location. Threat levels were developed to make the public aware of the nation's safety and to establish specific protocols that should be carried out by all the intelligence agencies, police, and emergency personnel during each of the threat levels. The National Security Agency (NSA) does not get much credit in this book because I don't know much about what they do and the same goes for all the other agencies. With that being said, Homeland Security is at the will of what the agencies choose to present to Homeland Security. The main problem with so many security organizations is secrets are meant to be kept secret and not shared with everybody. In essence, Homeland Security is like FEMA for a nationwide threat and response to whatever threat that affects the countries' threat levels.

The FBI gets most of the press during a peaceful threat level.

Much blame went around the various agencies over 9/11.

The FBI, more than any, could be blamed because of the number of responsibilities and duties they have allotted to them. Most of the 9/11 terrorists were caught on FBI surveillance cameras, reports, and actual FBI watches at some point before or during the attacks.

It is unclear if Homeland Security has picked up those responsibilities, if the FBI forwards any of these types of surveillance operations to Homeland Security or if the FBI just continues the same procedures without Homeland Security's knowledge.

The CIA, NSA, secret service, and other alphabet agencies along with police have equal number of questions on what gets sent to Homeland Security and what is not needed or purposely left out of reports. Most of these types of questions probably won't be answered because the art of security is the illusion that there is security. A great example was the January 6, 2021, assault on the Capitol Building: Full session of congress certifying the results of a national election and the security was minor. Limited riot gear with area police officers, volunteering to help once the breach of fencing was well on the way.

I visited the capitol many years ago and was surprised by the magnificent size of the building from the outside. The Capitol Building was tall, and the wings of congress were divided into house on one side and senate on the other. The combination of the width of the building and the height of the dome was very intimidating from the front of the building. There were security guards, metal detectors, and limited visitors allowed at one time. Tours were given off limited areas of the capitol because they were in session. I spotted my representative, and she grabbed our little group of about twelve visitors to the upper deck seating, and I remember Jesse Jackson's son was speaking in the house chamber at the podium. My representative was from the opposite party that I generally affiliate with, and she did not know me from Adam. She sat in front of me and asked what I could do for her, and thoughts crossed my mind for a second as she was a couple feet from the balcony edge. Then I said, "Keep doing what you are doing." Our group was allowed to stay another ten minutes, and we left. The point of the story is security is implied and breaches can be made by individuals that plan and are committed to do harm. The 9/11 was planned and committed by over nineteen people. The 2021 United States Capitol attack was half planned and most were committed. Homeland Security should be aware of these types of threats before committed people are able to execute their plans, no matter how well planned they are.

Taxpayers' money pay for all these security agencies and most of the agencies cross paths with one another in one area or another. To alleviate overlap in security, operations would save taxpayer dollars as well as confusion in covert operations. The need for informed, experienced, and decisive leadership in the security agencies is paramount.

Other areas that Homeland Security need to have oversight are the border patrol, the national guard, and the other branches of the military. Coordination concerning the war on drugs, the war on terror, the secretary of state, attorney general, and the rest of the cabinet members is important to allocate and receive intelligence from all areas of our vulnerable country.

This policy concerning Homeland Security is vast and dependent on the scale and scope of what is needed to fill the loose ends of what may be vulnerable. At the time of my typing of these words, the congress approved money for capitol security and money for Afghans that helped the US and their families to relocate to the US.

There are so many questions about this bill that I would ask. For instance, what improvements to security will be implemented and will they prevent another January 6 attack? How many Afghans helped the US? Which ones are allowed to come and which family members? Is any of the Afghans a security risk? Will security details need to be allocated for some, or will surveillance of others need to be assigned? Where are the Afghans settling and are they becoming US citizens? Do they speak English? The list of questions is endless.

This is a good time to suggest that you criticize your own policies before you make your final draft. Ask a lot of questions about your own ideas, and ask others for advice on issues that you are not familiar with from colleagues, interns, Google, and junk. Sometimes, policies do more harm than good, so make sure it will survive the test of scrutiny and give time frames and goal sets of the policy you choose to submit. Keep in mind: policies expire over the test of time. The constitution was written by rich old White guys, and I am pretty sure they did not intend on Americans having more than three guns per man, woman, and child. There were only thirteen colonies. With that being said, amendments help modify the constitution, and policies are expected to be modified over time as well. Follow-up of your policies will be crucial to make adjustments when needed, so you don't fall into a bad policy trap. Accountability will be discussed in a policy all its own later in this book.

Internet hacking and technology theft has made the country vulnerable to China, Russia, and other nations as well as individuals wanting to do harm to the United States. A large number of computer-savvy workers are needed for security firms for domestic as well as military companies.

Now for the size of this policy, I will have mostly high-end workers because of the number of decision-makers, career professionals, master degree jobs, PhD jobs, foreign consultants, technology professionals, and so on.

High-end salary jobs—100,000 jobs at $240,000 = $24 billion.
Upper-level salary jobs—200,000 jobs at $160,000 = $32 billion.
Foreign consultant jobs—50,000 jobs at $160,000 = $8 billion.
Technology jobs—100,000 jobs at $160,000 = $16 billion.
Lawyers—100,000 jobs at $160,000 = $16 billion.
FBI—100,000 jobs at $160,000 = $16 billion.
Blue-collar workers—250,000 jobs at $80,000 = $20 billion.

The grand total is 900,000 jobs for $132 billion.

The Homeland Security policy, like the other policies, is an aggressive approach to each of the areas that I have discussed in this book. The numbers of jobs and dollar amounts are going to vary in your own policy workup. The numbers also reflect an additional number of jobs on top of the jobs that are currently being funded. For instance, if there are 250,000 FBI agents, I am suggesting an additional 100,000 for a total of 350,000. I am also suggesting that other policies with FBI agents would be higher for those policies and not double up for current policy or existing agents. With that being said, existing agents can apply for the policy jobs, and their existing job can be posted for their replacement.

The cost of being secure is high, and additional tax dollars should be considered. Since September 11, 2021, there have been two tax cuts for high-end earners. There was no war tax like previous wars to offset the increased military and security costs. My $132-billion-a-year policy is a suggestion on top of what we have already done.

POLICY 6

International Peace and Trade

The United States has been considered the leader of the Free World since the World War II. After the 2016 election, many Americans realized that our status was rocked by an isolationist president, and then following the 2020 election, we had a fracture in our own democracy. The world will never see the United States as a leader of the Free World again. Many countries already had that feeling long before 2016. One hint can be found in a book written by Eugene Burdick and William Lederer in 1958 called *The Ugly American*, which they criticized the US foreign service and praised the soviet's approach to diplomacy. Now you can say they had a grudge against the US, but in my opinion, the similarities of the story line in the book and what followed in the US Vietnam War are unmistakable. Other examples are found in Central and South American countries that have embargos on socialist democracies (Bolivia and Venezuela). The US backing of the shah of Iran led to the US hostages in 1979 a failed rescue and then having Iraq invade Iran from 1980 to 1988. Subsequently, Saddam Hussein took Kuwait in payment of his work for the US. Well, the US and the international community under George H. Bush retook Kuwait and destroyed most of Iraq's regular army. Saddam Hussein was interviewed before his capture, and during the interview, he was asked why. Why did he invade Kuwait? His answer was "I was promised Kuwait." For context, George H. Bush used to be a CIA director before being VP under Reagan from

1980 to 1988, the same years as the Iraq-Iran War, eight years of Bill Clinton's no-fly zones in Iraq.

Bush Jr. came in and not even 9/11 could stop him from going to Iraq and capturing Saddam Hussein to be tried and hanged.

So, yes, the world knew before the citizens of the United States that we were not the leaders of the Free World.

In 2021, there came a new president from the old guard of the warring president of Obama, the former vice president and career politician, Joe Biden. In his first meetings with Europeans, the Europeans had no trust in what Joe had to say for fear that Trump would be back in 2024. No major commitments between the US and the Europeans could be addressed with any trust. In a strange way, the Covid-19 outbreak was a lucky break for foreign diplomacy because it bought time to delay everything in order to save face. The rally against a common enemy of China helped build a little trust as well as England's never-ending alliance with the United States.

Now that the reader has wrapped their mind around the free world business, international peace still needs to happen.

The United Nations was formed due to World War II and has the headquarters in New York City. There are five permanent members that have the ability to blackball any resolution they want. Twenty-member nations sit on the security council. Most of the nations in the world have offices in the UN to represent their countries in peace as well as in crisis. The five permanent members include: Russia, China, France, England, and the US. When George W. Bush decided to go to Iraq, he did not have support from the security council. The other four permanent members voted against it. Nevertheless, George W. Bush went ahead with the invasion. Being a permanent member is powerful. Russia invaded Afghanistan back in the '80s; they invaded Georgia on the first day of the Olympics so Putin could look in George W. Bush's eyes. Russia invaded Crimea and Chechnya. China has applied pressure in Sudan, Myanmar, Taiwan, Philippines, Vietnam, South Korea, North Korea, Japan, Venezuela, the US, and basically the whole world. France and England have had minor power plays in comparison to the three big brothers. All the other nations of the world either form alliances under one of the big brothers or try to hide from the alliances all together.

Before World War II, the United Kingdom was in every time zone. France had a bunch of colonies as well. Spain was weakened by civil war. Russia turned to Stalinism. Germany and Italy turned to fascism. The Ottoman Empire was starting its decline. Japan was expanding its empire in Asia. China was underdeveloped and had political factions warring one another. The United States was recovering from the worst financial depression the country has ever had.

The United Kingdom, France, and the United States sided with Hitler over Stalin in the Spanish Civil War. When Germany invaded Poland in 1939, the UK sided against Germany. Japan was expanding into China and was battling Stalin's troops in disputed areas. It wasn't until December 7, 1941, that the United States officially entered the war against Japan and its Axis allies, Germany, and Italy. The US and UK had to switch alliances with Stalin in order to coordinate containment and destruction of the Axis powers. Germany attacked Russia in order to prevent Russia from attacking first. After the war, Stalin returned to being our adversary. Europe was divided into east and west.

Today, the superpowers are the United States, Russia, China, and the European Union. England, the European Union. and the US belong to NATO. Russia and China are not members. With that being said, there is a power struggle with great powers aligning themselves militarily, economically, politically, educationally, and at the expense of their citizens as well as the countries that are being used for battle fields, resources, and by having some countries compromise alliances with other countries for fear of retaliation by one or more superpowers. To have world peace, we must be aligned with one another.

Communist China, Communist Russia, Democratic Socialist Europe with England, and the Capitalist United States must unite to be the United Countries of Planet Earth. Nuclear disarmament is easy under a united planet. Limited navy can also discourage any invasion attempts by any superpower. Regional boarders of responsibilities for economic stability for countries can be worked out in the

UN. Cultural and political views can be localized and not pushed upon people who do not believe in those views. Immigration can be more fluid for those who would prefer democratic socialism over communism or capitalism, or prefer Capitalism over Communism. India, Iran, and other religious and political countries can continue their ways as long as they don't pressure other people. Palestinians and Israelis can live in Israel as long as they don't criticize each other.

Remember when I said "the United States will never be called leader of the Free World again"? In a united earth, there is no one nation that leads. The security council that lost its vote 1–19 is not Democracy. If the US does not like the majorities' decision, then the US probably needs to reevaluate and compromise the view toward the majority. Keep in mind that George W. Bush's father, George H. Bush, got the security council's votes to invade Iraq. Going to it alone with small coalition was far costlier than a united coalition. Trump's economic war with China and shunning the Europeans in favor of North Korea and Russia was international political suicide for the US. Rogue dictators will not be tolerated, and unlike Genghis Khan, the Ottomans, the Romans, and the united countries of earth need to work together in a way that expands and improves what the British empire accomplished before World War II.

The European Union has created a mini-version of a global experiment, and if they can convince England to return to the union, it would be a good step forward. I actually thought England was wrong to join the EU in the first place. I was wrong. Russia and England should join the European Union. China and other Asian countries should join a union of their own. African Union can be expanded. The Americas can have their own union.

The key to the united planet will be convincing the superpowers to give up their power and accept the alliances of other countries. The United States has fifty states as well as US territories. People generally eat biscuits in the south, bagels in the northeast, pizza in Chicago, and no starches in the west. The states rely on the federal government to do the right thing and send representatives from all fifty states to ensure their representation. Not everyone wins, but most people do have food, shelter, work, religious freedom, political association or no politics at all. Personal security will still be needed to be applied. The goal is to remove the threat of war from one nation to another, let alone coalitions of war powers bumping against one another. This is obviously a long-term goal.

I have heard many peace-minded people talk about the long game and piece-by-piece diplomacy. It won't happen overnight and so on. Setting the long-game goal of a united-country planet is unlikely been seriously suggested. The short-term goals have been alliances, which only rub the countries on the other side of the alliance the wrong way, so they form alliances. The fact is we are on a planet whirling through space, and compared to the rest of wherever we are in space, our collective knowledge can't even begin to understand the significance of our existence. We have limited resources on this planet and need to gather resources from other planets and space debris in order to continue our civilization. Fighting one another over resources and wasting resources on weapons to protect our resources is counterintuitive to the long-term goal of any alliance.

Global trade has been beneficial in some cases and a hindrance in other cases. Overall, international trade is efficient and beneficial to the global economy. Less waste of goods and resources helps stretch out the availability to an ever-growing population. With that being said, how much steel is left in the planet? How much cropland is left? How much fresh drinking water is left? These are macroeconomic questions that need to be investigated, and there needs to be solutions made to transition to other resources if we need to live without a particular resource. The battery cars are bound to be temporary for the simple reason that there is limited silicone. Variations of minerals are being used to compensate for battery production. These resources are prime examples of how alliances will position against other alliances for control. The war in Vietnam was criticized for being a war over the oil in the South China Sea. Now China is building islands to put air bases in the same area that is disputed by area nations. Shared use and predetermined quantities of oil produced would eliminate the tensions, would limit the fuel to build defense bases, limit the use of fuel to fly military planes, and would limit the fuel for all other military vehicles to build and defend for decades.

Defense contractors can build peaceful engineered machines to help our search for resources on earth as well as off planet. Just like the health insurance companies can process universal health care so no jobs are lost, defense contractors can convert to other engineering needs to keep the high-end wage earners working. International trade is important on these types of goals, and discussions on climate change jobs are discussed later in this book, which have many examples of industrial jobs that can be created instead of building weapons of destruction.

Many jobs can be created in this policy of peace and tranquility. I will list a variety of jobs that can be helpful in transitioning from a planet of alliances against other alliances to a united planet of countries working together.

UN peacekeepers—1 million jobs at $80,000 = $80 billion.
Peace Corps—1 million jobs at $80,000 = $80 billion.
International trade paralegals—200,000 jobs at $160,000 = $32 billion.
International trade lawyers—100,000 jobs at $240,000 = $24 billion.
Trade accountants—200,000 jobs at $160,000 = $32 billion.
Statisticians—100,000 jobs at $80,000 = $8 billion.
Data analysts—100,000 jobs at $160,000 = $16 billion.
Economists—50,000 jobs at $160,000 = $8 billion.
International Army Corp of Engineers—100,000 jobs at $240,000 = $24 billion.
Disaster relief—50,000 jobs at $160,000 = $8 billion.
Foreign service—100,000 jobs at $160,000 = $16 billion.
Diplomats—20,000 jobs at $240,000 = $4.8 billion.
Interpreters—100,000 jobs at $160,000 = $16 billion.
Foreign Language Teachers—100,000 jobs at $80,000 = $8 billion.
Behavioral/cultural specialists for politicians and corporations and foreign service officers—50,000 jobs at $160,000 = $8 billion.
FBI agents—100,000 jobs at $160,000 = $16 billion.

The grand total is 3,370,000 jobs for $396.8 billion.

POLICY 7

Legal System

Partisan and nonpartisan judges should be vetted through a system similar to the military chain of command. For example, the US Supreme Court handles thousands of cases a year and can defer half of those cases that are lower-level cases to two lower supreme courts. The circuit courts would be underneath the lower supreme courts. There should be a ratio of no less than two-thirds of US supreme judges that come from these courts. This would keep the highest court from being hijacked by a potential 9–0 one-sided court. Three judges were placed in four years under Trump, and the court has leaned far right. This creates an anomaly of 60 percent of the country having 33 percent of the judges and 40 percent having 66 percent of the judges. Furthermore, the courts leading up to the circuit court need scrutiny and oversight.

Constitutional law should be expanded by modernizing the constitutional meaning of the law to be less vague. We need more judges empowered to rule on constitutional cases and less trivial cases that tie up the courts. Constitutional lawyers and paralegals will assist judges, politicians, NGOs, corporations, schools, law enforcement, the press, and the general public.

Data analysts can help assemble the data needed to help with the vetting of judges and other legal professionals. The analysts can also help government legal teams with the war on drugs, war on terror, war on poverty, war on police, war on immigration, and war on trade. Government contracts, laws, prosecutions, and sentencings are all areas that need improvements.

During Trump's four years, Trump had lawsuits against government agencies, corporations, countries, NGOs, individuals, and in turn, Trump was sued by all of the above. Lots of taxpayer dollars were spent representing both sides of most of the lawsuits.

I use Trump's four years a lot because he exposed a gap in many areas of our country that needs to be fixed. Our democracy is clearly fragile, and Trump's near-perfect dictatorship exposed the danger of all three branches of the government leaning one direction. A true democracy allows all ideals to be respected but never should the ideals be pushed against another's beliefs.

First example: abortion is legal, and many do not believe in abortion. Abortion is being challenged, but those people do not have to have an abortion if they don't believe in abortion.

Second example: the right to bear arms is the second amendment. No one is taking your right to protect yourself, but military-style weapons are unnecessary in a civilized country. We are not a third world nation, so we should not act like one. Have military weapons at gun clubs and not at the kitchen table.

Third example: taxes were hated, and the revolutionary war of 1776 was all about that. Legally, some people say we don't have to pay taxes, but I believe the constitution of 1789 placed taxes as a means to fund a well-regulated militia to protect businesses and enforce loan payments. The tax cuts from Reagan, George W. Bush, and Trump have caused deficits that threaten the protection of our republic. Legally, there should be some way to have a balanced budget by taxing the people that have received tax cuts even during the twenty-year unfunded wars in Afghanistan and Iraq.

Final example: liberalism being pushed on conservatives. It is not right. Liberals have no right to push social issues onto people that have a different value system. The Taliban in Afghanistan was the main party throughout that country. We went there and tried to force our western values after Bin Laden was long dead. It failed, and no one should be surprised. You can't have a conservative become a liberal, and a liberal can't become a conservative. If we want to keep a united states, we need to accept the other people's beliefs, but we should not have to be forced to believe the others' beliefs, and we should not be mean to other people's beliefs.

Judges—1,000 jobs at $240,000 = $240 million.
Lawyers—100,000 jobs at $160,000 = $16 billion.
Paralegals—200,000 jobs at $80,000 = $16 billion.
Data analysts—100,000 jobs at $160,000 = $16 billion.
International lawyers—100,000 jobs at $160,000 = $16 billion.
International paralegals—200,000 jobs at $80,000 = $16 billion.
International data analysts—200,000 jobs at $160,000 = $32 billion.
Professors/teachers—100,000 jobs at $160,000 = $16 billion.
Lower supreme court judges and support staff—2,000 jobs at $180,000 = $360 million.

The grand total is one million—3,000 jobs for $128.6 billion.

POLICY 8

Welfare and Medicaid to Work

In a capitalist society like ours, productivity is essential for growth. Headwinds to productivity include: inflation of the cost of inputs, lower morale of workers, and the reduction of workforce participation. All these headwinds can be reduced with policies that help get people off of unemployment and with a policy that would ease some people off of welfare and Medicaid. The unemployed is easy; people on welfare and Medicaid is the challenging part.

This policy suggestion is not intended to belittle or criticize the people that are in this category of economic gridlock. The capitalist model of economics does very little to accommodate or provide any practical solutions to this large portion of our population; that is, without any blame, unproductive and/or counterproductive. This policy addresses the headwinds of productivity by lowering the cost of the safety net (welfare checks, food stamps, etc.), increases the moral of the potential workforce, and increases the workforce participation.

Welfare and Medicaid are common targets on the right. The solution is cut the programs—not helpful and not practical economically. Removing the only income of millions of Americans would cause a recession, if not worse. Maslow's hierarchy of needs lists a basic need of food, shelter, and health.

A step-up from the basic needs can be characterized as productivity of oneself, which includes work, education, family, and spirituality. For many people, spirituality is the first step, and for all intents and purposes, both steps should be the first step. In this country or any capitalist country, spirituality is not represented on the economic spreadsheet; however, spirituality is part of a majority of basic needs as food, shelter, and health. Spirituality is part of the morale of most workers as well as most people on welfare and Medicaid. With that being said, a policy to transition as many people off of welfare and Medicaid is better than a flat-out cut and is better than the status quo of keeping people locked in an economic cage (zookeeping people).

I worked for Goodwill Industries in Florida and found it rewarding to see the increased donations and increased job opportunities year after year. Of course, Florida is a state that is fast-growing and cannot compare with some northern states that have been losing populations for various reasons. In addition to the growth of the job opportunities, there were handicapped people who were being helped to help themselves in everyday situations that we take for granted and providing part-time work for them to feel productive in their lives. I visited one of these facilities that had production lines providing packaging for sprinkler heads and perfumes by handicapped workers and for private companies. A lady with traumatic brain injury and a man who was blind even assisted in our dispatch office for home pickups of donations. I strongly suggest everyone to take a tour of your nearest Goodwill or any company that provides these services. The joy and spirit of these workers to have the opportunity to feel needed was inspiring.

Another life example I wish to share with you is a great example on how the current system of government layout needs reform. I had two friends that were handicapped—one from school and one I met through the other friend. They both had similar problems with one side of their bodies having weakness in their muscles. The school friend worked part-time, lived at home, and wanted to work more hours so he could get his own place, but the government would cut all the monthly checks and all the health benefits. Well, the checks were not the problem. He could work more. The problem was the health benefits, which he needed because of the occasional seizures he would have. The other friend had worked hard all his life to minimize his handicap, which, at first, I quite honestly did not even realize he had a handicap. He worked out at the gym every day, worked thirty or more hours a week, and lived at home. The difference in the severity did not prevent the two from working, but the severity of the one young school friend needing health care while the other was not as concerned about health care was the difference.

Guess which friend had the most confidence?

Both friends did have emotional issues as they got older, which neither of my friends went to counseling that I am aware of. Neither of them participated in the Goodwill program that had counselors working, counseling, and providing positive social support every day. This positive caring for one another is another step in Maslow's hierarchy of needs that leads to self-actualization.

My policy would add two million social workers spread across this country. They would help in every aspect of our society: police departments, schools, hospitals, social services departments, military, veterans, nursing homes, local governments, and wherever I can't think of. These social workers will need to be trained and vetted to provide a uniform set of guidelines that respect the people they are assisting, guiding, and helping. Notice how there was no mention of people on welfare. Our society needs to be accommodative to the proposed policy. People not on welfare are sometimes one step away from welfare, so providing the resources to curb people from getting on welfare as well as after welfare is beneficial to the overall goal of increased productivity.

Teachers are huge parts of every policy, and education policies will be discussed in the later chapters. Education is essential for the common good of our society to communicate and educate the work force of the future, which is now. Teachers and counselors will teach people how to be productive without the social safety net or with a minimum safety net. Trade school teachers are also needed more than ever because they have more hands-on training, which provides great confidence for people who are not sure of their skill set.

Tutoring schools like Sylvan Learning Inc. and others are beneficial in targeting needs of students as they need to be brought up to standards that are set by the school systems.

Psychologists and psychiatrists are used in big businesses and social media to sell more goods. They are rarely used to increase the productivity of the individual or focus on the effects of the psychology of the corporation's effects on society. Mental illness is not easy to diagnose, and often, people are just a little crazy and may not need fixing. Group therapy for everybody may be easier to take out the stereotype and provide community understanding and support no matter if you are Christian, Muslim, transgender, straight, White, Black, mixed, educated or uneducated, poor, or rich. The movie *the Breakfast Club* had a variety of kids essentially having a group therapy session more than a detention. The result was a better understanding of one another without giving up your basic ideals. The prom queen is still the prom queen. The football player is still the football player.

Job placement counselors and workforce trainers can help Tech and big business acquire and train people who were on welfare or Medicaid as well as retirees who may want to reenter the workforce. Many times, there have been early retirements, and that lowers the participation rate of workers. Providing jobs for the elderly can be beneficial to productivity if they are placed on the right jobs.

Do we really need charities to help the homeless in this country? Or can we just develop a housing policy using people on welfare, Medicaid, retired, or rich to provide the housing? Donating to the arts in Los Angeles, Chicago, and New York will not help the artists in the south and neither will all the other charities. Ironically, the red states preach the charities over social programs while the south relies on social programs percentage-wise over charity. Minimum wage of 7.25 an hour is not even close to what most low-wage workers make now. Fifteen dollars an hour raises most working poor out of poverty.

By providing jobs to welfare and Medicaid recipients, payroll taxes will be collected from their labor. The increased tax revenue will help pay for future costs related to transitioning workers back to work. Also, once the numbers go down, the overstaffing can help transition immigrants to work as we immigrate more people to grow the country from the bottom to the top.

Remember, most of the people who are to be helped with this policy will need to help themselves as well as participate in programs designed to empower and motivate their transition to productivity. Many of these people have only known this way of life and may even have been multigenerational in nature. Patience and hard work will facilitate most, but some will not be capable. Solutions for the later must be developed to finally remove welfare from one of the richest countries in the world. The social workers at the beginning of this policy was, as you can remember, designed to encompass all of our society to function together so that we don't have large numbers of people and families falling behind.

Accountability for all these jobs and this policy are of the utmost necessity to limit fraud and abuse. With that being said, accountants, statisticians, economists, and administrators will need to be hired for the implementation of this bold policy.

My suggested cost for this policy is to tackle the problems head-on and would reduce over time as the people come off welfare. Again, most of these jobs would transfer into other policy needs as well as maintain a level of support to keep people off welfare all together.

Administrators—10,000 jobs at $160,000 = $1.6 billion.
Economists—10,000 jobs at $160,000 = $1.6 billion.
Data analysts—50,000 jobs at $160,000 = $8 billion.
Mental health professionals—50,000 jobs at $160,000 = $8 billion.
Statisticians—100,000 jobs at $80,000 = $8 billion.
Counselors/teachers—1 million jobs at $80,000 = $80 billion.
Social workers—2 million jobs at $80,000 = $160 billion.

The grand total is 3.21 million jobs for $267.2 billion.

NOTES

POLICY 9

Infrastructure

Infrastructure by my standards is defined as public works projects that include dams, roads, bridges, other transportation systems, water systems, sewer systems, power grids, and the communications grid. All these require state, local, federal, and private sector money to pay for it. Most of these projects take up to ten years from start to finish.

Obama had his 2009 infrastructure deal that required new projects for the money. This created a problem for some local governments that had cost overruns on existing projects, and there was reduced tax revenue from the 2008 housing crisis. Most of the Obama projects were small and created temporary jobs. Planning took most of the front-end years and many states with low populations found no real need to use the money for anything.

The next infrastructure bill to be presented to the senate for actual voting came in 2021. In twelve years, Dubai completed trillions of dollars in infrastructure. In twelve years, China completed ten new cities that could hold two million people each. In twelve years, China built islands in the South China Sea and built air bases on them. In twelve years, the European Union started to stabilize its euro and its political structure. In twelve years, Elon Musk built the battery car, built charging stations, built solar shingles for homes, built space ships that took off every month, built a boring company to build his hyperlink transportation system, and he developed AI for cars and robots.

The so-called richest country in the world does next to nothing to provide infrastructure. When economic crisis happens, politicians throw infrastructure money at the problem, which is the wrong time to do it. Cutting taxes is also done when taxes should be increased to pay for responses. Consequently, the national debt goes up expediential.

Infrastructure must be planned for the future growth and not for theatrics during an economic crisis. Some politicians say, "We don't need infrastructure because the economy is going good, and we don't want to borrow money or raise taxes." The fact is, low-interest rates by the fed, low-bond rates, and minor tax increase can help the economy sustain itself for years into the future. For example: if you plant a tree, water it, and maintain it, the tree will grow and provide fruit if it is a fruit tree. If you plant a tree, leave it alone, and expect the weather to provide for it, then it will either live or die. If it lives, it won't provide the same amount as the trees that have well maintenance.

This policy provides jobs for infrastructure to try to catch up with the slack in government's failure to provide sufficient infrastructure for an industrialized country. Productivity is a capitalist necessity, and having quality infrastructure provides the most productive way for supply chains to flow with minimal resistance.

Many private industry jobs are available to build all of what is needed, and whenever there is a short fall in contractors, the Army Corp of Engineers can fill that void.

Waste and fraud will have to be monitored in this policy and the Government Accounting Office (GAO) and the Congressional Budget Office (CBO) can help with the budget numbers.

Red states and low-population states will usually push back on these types of policies because they see no advantage to it. Providing high-speed rail to Florida can help tourism in Florida. Using tar sands from North Dakota and processed in Texas can help fuel the heavy equipment and provide building materials for roads. Ohio has many factories that supply infrastructure materials and equipment. Much like Boeing aircraft, many of the states have different industries that provide for other states, and focusing on those industries and states will make it easier to pass an infrastructure bill.

Targeting which systems need to be fixed by state and region will lead to planning and scheduling of the projects. Setting up four or five regions would help target the most needed projects on the front-end and would also disperse the large sums across the country evenly as far as geographically.

GAO and CBO staff—5,000 jobs at $80,000 = $400 million.
Administrators—10,000 jobs at $160,000 = $1.6 billion.
CPAs—10,000 jobs at $240,000 = $2.4 billion.
Economists—10,000 jobs at $160,000 = $1.6 billion.
Planners, designers, and inspectors—40,000 jobs at $160,000 = $6.4 billion.
Data analysts—25,000 jobs at $160,000 = $4 billion.
Accountants—50,000 jobs at $160,000 = $8 billion.
Statisticians—50,000 jobs at $80,000 = $4 billion.
Lawyers—20,000 jobs at $160,000 = $3.2 billion.
Paralegals—50,000 jobs at $80,000 = $4 billion.
Computer techs—20,000 jobs at $160,000 = $3.2 billion.
Army Corps of Engineers—100,000 jobs at $160,000 = $16 billion.
Engineers—20,000 jobs at $240,000 = $4.8 billion.
Mechanics—20,000 jobs at $160,000 = $3.2 billion.
Electricians—20,000 jobs at $160,000 = $3.2 billion.
Welders—20,000 jobs at $160,000 = $3.2 billion.
Other trades—100,000 jobs at $80,000 = $8 billion.
Basic labor—200,000 jobs at $80,000 = $16 billion.

The grand total is 770,000 jobs for $93.2 billion.

POLICY 10

Climate Change

The world has been concerned about climate change since the end of the nineteenth century. The mid to late 1800s was the industrial revolutions birth. The Great Smog of London was worse than it ever was, and the start of truly caring about climate change began by increased scientific studies and recording of temperatures around the world.

World War I and World War II put a pause in pollution concern, but the advent of the nuclear technology would curb some of the global demands for energy through coal. Oil, gas, and nuclear energy would finish the twentieth century as the primary fuel sources. With that being said, these alternatives to coal have caused environmental damage in certain parts of the world, and coal is still used in third world countries as well as in China.

The first twenty-one years of the twenty-first century would prove to be beneficial for the scientists, politicians, and citizens who have begged for policies to try and combat global warming / climate change. Windmills, solar panels, carbon filters, battery powers, and hydrogen energy have started to replace coal-burning turbines and gas-powered cars. Nuclear power plants have had some problems leading to the shutdown of some plants around the world. Geothermal energy and water-powered turbines have also helped in these endeavors to steer away from pollution-making energy.

Fusion reactors and improvements in battery technology and microchips have accelerated the transition off of the bad energy sources. The need for even more scientists, engineers, physicists, mechanics, electricians, computer techs, and professors are of high demand. We need millions around the world of highly intelligent people to continue our advancement in our new revolution into the twenty-second and twenty-third centuries. The politicians and the people who disregard this future will be left behind. No matter if a country is capitalist or communist, cheap energy is clean energy.

Fisheries, tree planting, and lab-created meats and vegetables will help with food supplies as well as curb over farming of these limited resources.

Developing a twenty-year ration ban on commercial fishing would restock our oceans with future food supplies. Sportfishing as well as targeted commercial fishing can be continued where there is abundant predators and large populations of sea life. Much like the oil industry subsidies, commercial fishermen can be subsidized to teach the new system of fishing, assist in collection of garbage in the sea, assist scientists with monitoring the fish populations as well as everything else related to the oceans. Retraining into other occupations and possibly creating a civilian-type coast guard for young and old fishermen who love the sea can help calm the displeasure of regulating the industry.

Trump had pushed a plan to plant one trillion trees worldwide. Plant-for-the-Planet was founded at Grimaldi Forum, Monaco, in 2018. It was formerly called the Billion Tree Campaign. Continued efforts in this project will require additional jobs to help plant seeds to trees. Maintenance of those forests was not discussed other than criticism that California failed to keep up federal lands. The whole continent of Australia burned for one year, so improved maintenance of our planet should be a major concern.

Lab-created food has become abundant in grocery stores and in fast-food restaurants. Like everything else we consume on this planet, there is scarcity of minerals, and we need to constantly be aware of the long-term solutions of these new food sources. Processing and filtering the oceans, rivers, lakes, and wastewater into fresh drinking water should continue to improve, but the costs of these processing facilities are not very productive, yet we have no choice. We cannot live without water. Water shortages are frequent and have created dry conditions, resulting in increased fires.

Much like the new city development policy, existing cities need to build energy-efficient buildings and transportation systems to limit the destruction of our planet. Buying unnecessary things would also limit the pollution and resources needed to make the unneeded items. Recycling of garbage is a major problem, and just fishing it out of the sea is no good if cities around the world are continuing to dump more into the oceans.

New technology needs to be developed to stabilize our planet temperature, such as a thermostat in a house. No matter how the problem has presented itself, we must stabilize the temperature. or else. we will watch our planet turn into a desert with dead oceans.

Scientists—100,000 jobs at $240,000 = $24 billion.
Engineers—100,000 jobs at $240,000 = $24 billion.
Army Corps of Engineers—100,000 jobs at $160,000 = $16 billion.
Administrators—100,000 jobs at $160,000 = $16 billion.
Professors—100,000 jobs at $160,000 = $16 billion.
Planners, designers, and inspectors—100,000 jobs at $160,000 = $16 billion.
Fishermen—100,000 jobs at $160,000 = $16 billion.
Coast guards/civilians—50,000 jobs at $160,000 = $8 billion.
Teachers/counselors—100,000 jobs at $80,000 = $8 billion.
Forest service—100,000 jobs at $80,000 = $8 billion.
Firefighters/paramedic—100,000 jobs at $80,000 = $8 billion.
Disaster relief—100,000 jobs at $80,000 = $8 billion.
Tree planters—200,000 jobs at $80,000 = $16 billion.
Mechanics—100,000 jobs at $160,000 = $16 billion.
Electricians—100,000 jobs at $160,000 = $16 billion.
Welders—100,000 jobs at $160,000 = $16 billion.
Other trades—100,000 jobs at $80,000 = $8 billion.
Basic labor—500,000 jobs at $80,000 = $40 billion.
Data analysts—100,000 jobs at $160,000 = $16 billion.

Accountants—100,000 jobs at $160,000 = $16 billion.
Statisticians—100,000 jobs at $80,000 = $8 billion.
Computer techs—200,000 jobs at $160,000 = $32 billion.
Lab techs—200,000 jobs at $160,000 = $32 billion.
Lawyers—50,000 jobs at $160,000 = $8 billion.
Paralegals—100,000 jobs at $80,000 = $8 billion

The grand total is 3.1 million jobs for $400 billion.

Four hundred billion dollars is just the labor, educating, training, and equipping the workers. The building and production costs will have to be funded through billing and consumption taxes. I remember a joke from years ago saying, "The next thing you know, they will jar air and sell it." I remember when there was a talk about bottling water and selling it. I thought, *who would buy water when you can drink it out of the faucets and water fountains?* Well, freshwater is more of a concern nowadays, and the quality of the local water systems is always in question.

The military budget has always been high, and the addition of a monster policy like this is actually more important than additional military. Actually, the control over water and food sources is a national security necessity that should not be overlooked.

Education System Part 1

Education reform has been talked about for years. Various types of reforms have been implemented across the country. Some work, some don't work, and some are inconclusive. Having a clear understanding of what is needed to teach our children from birth to college and beyond will require a comprehensive analysis of social and economic factors.

The world has various success stories in education, but the political and economic structures of those countries generally do not line up with ours. With that being said, various parts of the country can have success with their way of successfully educating their citizens. The other parts of the country would need their own system that aligns with their way of thinking. Our complicated country refuses to have a one-size-fits-all education system. School districts across the country could choose from a list of no less than five systems for their education system. There should be approval of the system chosen with the state and notify the US Department of Education. Having five options gives communities the flexibility to rally behind a system of their choice, which improves participation of parents and teachers in the process of educating our children.

Early childhood development varies in every child, which is a problem for planning for early education systems. Preschool, pre-kindergarten, first-grade, and even second-grade children can be on wide ranges of understanding. Labeling of what age for what grade has been a contentious subject for many teachers, administrators, and parents. The children at these ages don't really care, but as they get older, it becomes an issue. To solve this problem, tutoring and split-year advancement programs can get the students back to where they need to be as well as help those smart students accelerate their education going forward with same age students.

For example: A four-year-old kid is smart enough to go into first grade. They take the first half in preschool and the second half in first grade. Another kid is six years old and has a hard time with first grade, so the kid repeats first grade for a half year, then second grade in the second half, then second grade in the first half, and then third, and so on.

Summer school with tutoring can provide a catch-up opportunity for those who can, but the planning of an additional framework to keep the students from falling too far behind is prudent and keeps kids of the same age together in the split classes. The advantage, too, is if the student were to have even more trouble, they would only lose another half year. Students failing a couple grades of school might only be behind one year instead of two, provided they work at catching up with their studies. There's a lot to unpack with this, which is why there should be studies into this problem.

Over the years, there has been a transition in certain school districts to provide students with the option to take community college classes as well as trade school classes while in their junior and senior years. I would go all the way and increase middle school and early-year high school classes curriculums so the students can transfer to college or a trade school after their tenth grade.

Community colleges have added some trade schools and certificate programs to the curriculum and increasing these trade class options will help the country increase the number of skilled workers that companies have been struggling to find. Having a wide range of options for people to decide what they want to do when they grow up is beneficial for productivity of the workforce, which is good for the capitalist system.

Administrators—20,000 jobs at $160,000 = $3.2 billion.
Planners and educators—50,000 jobs at $160,000 = $8 billion.
Professors—10,000 jobs at $160,000 = $1.6 billion.
Trade school teachers—50,000 jobs at $160,000 = $8 billion.
Teachers and counselors—150,000 jobs at $80,000 = $12 billion.
Teacher's assistants—100,000 jobs at $80,000 = $8 billion.
Tutors—200,000 jobs at $80,000 = $16 billion.
Data analysts—50,000 jobs at $160,000 = $8 billion.
Accountants—50,000 jobs at $160,000 = $8 billion.
Statisticians—50,000 jobs at $80,000 = $4 billion.
Preschool teachers—100,000 jobs at $80,000 = $8 billion.
Day care workers—100,000 jobs at $80,000 = $8 billion.
Basic staff—100,000 jobs at $80,000 = $8 billion.

The grand total is 1.03 million jobs for $100.8 billion.

Education System Part 2

Energy-efficient schools should be required whenever they are renovated or built. Multistory buildings with solar, wind, and other forms of climate-friendly architecture can actually produce more energy, which makes it viable to pay for upgrades and maintenance over the duration of the life of the buildings. Many people always bring up outsourcing, and this is a possible avenue in addition to government policies to use fed rate interest rates to borrow toward education infrastructure.

Internet classes have been increasing over the years to accommodate students in rural areas, returning students, refresher classes, and working students. These classes have a wide range of costs and a wide range of certifications if any. Accountability of these classes should be taken seriously, and the schools offering these classes should be very transparent on the class accreditation.

Life has its ups and downs, and to offset some people's downfalls in high school education, GED classes are available to those who choose to receive a high school equivalency that haven't been able to, for one reason or another, finish high school. Outreach to citizens of all ages to offer classes either for work or for their own benefit should be done to help the general well-being of the country through basic education of our whole country. In addition, various classes can be offered in specific areas of interest; examples include aerobics, self-defense, sports, constitutional training, foreign languages, CPR, lifeguard, safety, and many other subject matters.

Teachers and counselors need training, and additional schools to qualify more teachers will be needed to accommodate the expansion of the education systems.

The broad range of teachers and counselors needed is covered in every segment of our society. Some examples of these jobs will help educate teachers and counselors for welfare to work, law enforcement, constitutional training, law school, foreign service, paramedic, nurses, doctors, mental health, social service, preschool, high school, aerobics, music, self-defense, and so on. With that being said, professors and administrators will also be needed.

Administrators—25,000 jobs at $160,000 = $4 billion.
Educators and planners—75,000 jobs at $160,000 = $12 billion.
Professors—25,000 jobs at $160,000 = $4 billion.
Teachers/counselors—200,000 jobs at $80,000 = $16 billion.
Teacher assistants—100,000 jobs at $80,000 = $8 billion.
Tutors—100,000 jobs at $80,000 = $8 billion.
Preschool teachers—50,000 jobs at $80,000 = $4 billion.
Basic staff—100,000 jobs at $80,000 = $8 billion.

The grand total is 675,000 jobs for $64 billion.

POLICY 13

Social Security and Tax Law

Social security is a polarizing subject, and the people that fight it the most are more likely in the system or will be in the future. Taxes are not easy to understand, and social security is the most confusing, yet it is the most beneficial for the stability of our economy during recessions. Funding for social security is received every month through payroll deductions. The drama of social security running out of money is just that—drama.

Social security can be modified by congress, signed by the president, and then implemented within thirty days. No big deal. The modification that is the easiest is raising the threshold from $137,000 a year to $1 million. Companies that have employees making more than $137,000 a year can afford the extra deductions and so can the employees making that amount of money.

With that being said, I would plan on a policy to reduce the employer side on by 3 percent to give small businesses a small break but the threshold does raise from $137,000 to $1 million. In addition, I would raise the threshold on the employee side to $20 million. The first $1 million would be 7.5% employee and 4.5% employer. The next $19 million would have no employer contribution, but there would be a 4.5% employee contribution. These percentages include the OASI, DI, and HI. The revenue shores up social security and provides additional funds for more services and increased payouts.

Accountability is a policy in itself, but it should be recognized in every policy you create. Social security is a major target for politicians as opposed to the military budget that clearly has problems yet receives next to no scrutiny. Other than cost of living increases, social security has had very little adjustments in contrary to the defense budgets getting tens of billions more each year.

Businesses with employees making less than $137,000 a year will save 3% wage contributions. Now, some companies match that amount in employee IRAs. If companies don't have the IRAs now, they can afford them. Tax laws have been changed almost every year in contrast to social security tax laws. Many of the changes resulted in a wealth gap increase. The republican tax reductions from 1980 to now have reduced the tax burden on the wealthy from 70% to 37%. The effects of the reduction clearly hampered job creation as well as reduced the middle class.

Reagan tax cuts started the ball rolling in 1981 by reducing the high-end tax revenue that pays for our military and everything else from 70% to 50%. The devastation was quick and resulted in the Tax Equity and Fiscal Responsibility Act of 1982. It was called the biggest tax hike since the postwar. The walk back in taxes in this law directly affected the middle-class workers, which caused the beginning of the crushing of the middle class. The republican congress bill North American Free Trade Agreement (NAFTA), signed by Bill Clinton, destroyed any hope of saving the middle class.

Reagan was not finished giving himself and other rich people tax breaks. In 1986, the Tax Reform Act of 1986 was passed, reducing the top earners tax burden that paid for our military and other government services from 50% to 28%. Remember, the first 20 percent caused an emergency to tax the middle class the following years. Now, he reduces 22 percent on top wage earners. What was he thinking? Inflation was through the roof because of all the money in the system. Taxes on cigarettes, gas, alcohol, groceries, and local taxes had to go up to pay for shortfalls in government services. The consumption taxes as well as the inflation affected the lower and middle classes the most.

George H. Bush became president, and he referred to the top-down economics of Reagan as "voodoo economics." The economy and jobs buckled under Reaganomics under H. Bush.

Bill Clinton became president, and him and the republican congress created surpluses by not spending as much by cutting military-spending, welfare to work, a modest increasing tax on the rich, and job creation policies like the one that paid for one hundred thousand police officers to communities that were in need of more officers but lacked the funding. That's one hundred thousand middle-class jobs. During his eight years in office, there were wars, but they were not as major as the other wars. Iraq had no-fly zones. Kosovo had a United Nations-backed war with US suppling the most troops. Somalia and other skirmishes could be referred to as police action wars. Vietnam was often called a police action, but it was a war and was fought like one some days and not so much other days. The key to the Clinton years was his use of the United Nations, which saved the US in military boots on ground even if it cost us more in diplomatic dues at the United Nations as well as bribes to heads of governments to keep the peace.

NAFTA, like I said before, finished off the middle class. So when the son of George H. Bush came into office, there was a reduction of wealth in the middle class, and young people were looking to make less than their parents before them. September 11, 2001, attacks on our country destroyed any chance of a domestic policy for years to come. The military became the only thing that mattered for all of W. Bush's eight years in office.

George W. Bush did pass his Bush tax cuts in 2001 and 2003. Oddly enough, there seems to be a constant republican strategy of reducing taxes and raising more budgets for military-spending at the same time. Years ago whenever a war would come about, there would be a war tax to pay for the higher cost needed to fund the wars. Talk about increasing deficit spending. I will give you examples:

In 1979, Iran became an enemy of the United States when the shah of Iran was ousted and the US Embassy was overtaken by Iranians, which held US hostages. Jimmy Carter did not feel it was right to start a war right before a US election, so Reagan won, and in

1980, the United States allowed Saddam Hussein to invade Iran. The United States did not need to deal with Iran for now. So in 1981, Reagan reduced the taxes on the high-end from 70% to 50%. Then the military budgets started to climb for missiles in space technology and to build against the Soviet Union. While building military year after year, Reagan drops the high-end 22% more in 1986.

In September 11, 2001, George W. Bush was president. He sent troops to Afghanistan and then cut taxes on the rich in 2001. Then he decided to invade Iraq and continued his tax cuts in 2003. Meanwhile, hundreds of billions of dollars were being spent in Afghanistan and Iraq.

Obama came into office for eight years and continued the Bush tax cuts and continued the wars in Iraq and Afghanistan. Obamacare was his legacy besides being the first African-American president. Job creation was minimal because of the lack of policies allowed on the floor of the house and senate. Only Obamacare was effective in helping some people get insurance where they wouldn't have been able to before. The front-end costs offset any gains during his terms in office. The benefits of the law started taking root under Trump by the governors of most states helping to continue what clearly helped reduce costs on health care.

The Trump tax cut had zero effect because all the money that was not collected for military-spending went into the stock market, and businesses that benefited wound up doing stock buybacks, which create zero jobs. Trump's economic war with China did bring some jobs back to the states, which did lower the unemployment rate, even his anti-immigrant stance did not slow the immigrants from coming to the border at first. Then there was a small drop in immigrants, which caused some lower-waged jobs to open up. Then the Covid-19 started ravaging the world and immigrants started to rush the border to get vaccines in 2020 and 2021.

Joe Biden comes into office, and he get the vaccines out to other countries as well as our own, get us out of Afghanistan, and he fought for a 3.5 trillion-dollar infrastructure bill that would put millions of people to work over the next eight years as well as taxes the rich modestly. Stimulus checks were given to cushion some of the financial strain of the Covid outbreak. Child credits were given out, which reduced child poverty in the United States by half.

Taxes pay for stuff. Our country cannot survive with a 28 percent tax bracket on high-end earners like Reagan did in 1986.

Tax policy should be revised to try to balance the budget or have surplus like Bill Clinton, and the republican congress was able to do years ago. Try not to have wars; we can't afford them. If we have to go to war, we should have the UN and allies with us, like Bill and George H. did. We should have a limited war tax if we have to ramp up more than what our volunteer army already has to deter aggressors. We need to have more accountability for our defense-spending, which is far more than what we pay out for social security.

To conclude, this policy can be split up into a social security policy, and then tax law revisions can be adjusted to try to balance the budget. Cutting programs or spending other than military would be counter-intuitive to our need to restore the domestic economy of the United States. I also apologize for the extra discussion about the different presidents, but there needed to be some context behind what each president did and what the economic impact caused.

Administrators—20,000 jobs at $160,000 = $3.2 billion.
Fraud detectives—20,000 jobs at $160,000 = $3.2 billion.
Planners and budgeters—20,000 jobs at $160,000 = $3.2 billion.
CPAs and auditors—100,000 jobs at $160,000 = $16 billion
Data analysts—50,000 jobs at $160,000 = $8 billion.
Statisticians—100,000 jobs at $80,000 = $8 billion.
Tax accountants—100,000 jobs at $80,000 = $8 billion.
Accountants—100,000 jobs at $80,000 = $8 billion.
Lawyers—50,000 jobs at $160,000 = $8 billion.
Paralegals—100,000 jobs at $80,000 = $8 billion.
General staff—100,000 jobs at $80,000 = $8 billion.

The grand total is 760,000 jobs for $72 billion.

POLICY 14

Accountability and Balanced Budgets

Political oversight of the government needs to be run by an independent organization. The self-policing of the government with political oversight committees chaired and run by the politicians that in some cases need overseeing is not transparent at all. The politicians used to abide by a code of ethics and respect for one another's opinions even when they disagreed. In the last few years, there has been hostility that blew up when Trump became president. The president leads by example and is the figurehead of the US and what it stands for. Attacking democrats and their families every day and having the republican leadership allow the hate to persist has caused a permanent rift in the country.

Our leaders in this republic were elected to represent our laws and constitutional rights. They are supposed to be honorable and forthright. There is no question that democrats and republicans have polar opposite views. There are some things that both parties can agree on, but there is no honor in name-calling and threats to one another on both sides of the isle. There is no honor in spreading rumors you know are not true. Mitch McConnell is a prime example of a politician that refuses to do anything democratic, but he does not lie about things that are obvious. He plays a mean politician and is good at doing nothing and getting away with it. Trump's wall could have been put in a defense bill, but he refused to do it.

Congressional hearings are ongoing, and the results of those hearings are usually inconclusive. Political leverage and favors are transacted to protect one another from any serious fallout. Occasionally, a politician goes down in disgrace. But most are free to do what they want or bow out of reelections. One example was when Richard Burr and Dianne Feinstein were accused of insider trading. Well, Richard Burr announced his plans to not run for reelection. Dianne Feinstein was obviously speaking kindly to the republicans in committee meetings when they still had the senate majority. She never announced if she would not run for reelection. Democrats barely won the senate back.

Again, the transparency is broken in Washington. The defense bills are the most outrageous in unaccountability. There hasn't been a balance of the books in the Pentagon for decades. The GAO and the CBO have the capability to get the budget balanced in the Pentagon as well as all the governments budgets. Accountability of the budgets has been left unchecked and has only been a criticism on the floor of the congress for politicians, just like social security has been a political football when all that has to happen is a journal entry and collection from rich people who have more money than they know what to do with. Bitcoin and all the other digital currencies were developed just for the rich to put their money somewhere else and not have accountability for it.

This policy of accountability would save and find billions of tax-payer dollars. We can balance the budget and create surplus money for infrastructure-spending for the following year. There would be more trust in the government if the politicians are held to a higher standard. There will be more trust in the other policies that are created, and there would be more trust in the people who implement the policies. The beneficiaries of policies can also be held to standards, which brings trust to the system.

Throughout this book, I have mentioned accountability, and it should be part of every policy that is created. For this policy, there needs to be a structural overhaul of our current failed system.

NGO participants—200,000 jobs at $160,000 = $32 billion.
NGO workers—300,000 jobs at $80,000 = $24 billion.
GAO workers—100,000 jobs at $160,000 = $16 billion.
CBO workers—100,000 jobs at $160,000 = $16 billion.
Administration personnel for the various departments (education, defense, social security, Homeland Security, etc.)—1 million jobs at $80,000 = $80 billion.
State and local government employees—1 million jobs at $80,000 = $80 billion.
Auditors—100,000 jobs at $160,000 = $16 billion
Lawyers—200,000 jobs at $160,000 = $32 billion
Paralegals—300,000 jobs at $80,000 = $24 billion
Fraud detectives—100,000 jobs at $160,000 = $16 billion.

The grand total is 3.4 million jobs for $336 billion.

CONCLUSION

Trickle-down economics with tax cuts and the trade policies that shipped jobs overseas for cheaper labor costs caused recessions and wealth gaps. True investment in this country's infrastructure has not happened in decades. Joe Biden pushed the infrastructure policies in his first term. Tax cuts have an inverse effect on infrastructure-spending even though the stock market did well. Understanding these facts will help people who will form policies in the future.

Job creation creates bottom-up economics, which increases sales, profits, and tax revenue. A shortage of job growth limits everything except the inflationary outlays and population growth. The lack of policies that help the domestic health of this country weakened our education system, immigration system, and many other social policies that have been tearing this country apart.

Thank you for your commitment to searching for policies that can help create millions of middle-class jobs. With that being said, the policies you make today will have a shelf life of relevance. A crime bill in the 1990s is not effective in 2020s. Remember, the policies that are created are to fix problems like welfare or overbudgeting waste. Once the problems are solved, the policies become irrelevant and need to be replaced or illuminated in some cases.

These example policies were just suggestions and can be reduced or expanded depending on the needs that are requiring attention. The policies will have to pass the congress, which requires finding good parts for democrats and republicans at the same time. Targeting only democrat or only republican policies will not work. Examples include republicans' policies of doing nothing for decades set our domestic health back for decades. Democrats voting on hundreds of bills that never got voted on are failed attempts to truly do good work. Forcing republicans to form policies with the democrats creates policies and bills that can be agreed upon to help the country invest in itself.

Taxes pay for the military and domestic outlays. Cutting taxes limits our domestic goals and increases our deficits. The excessive military-spending is not funded and adds to the deficits.

The jobs created also increase the demand for other jobs in retail, services, and manufacturing.

NOTES

Most people my age could write a miniseries about their lives—who we are, where we grew up, what our ups and downs were.

My usual intro to someone new is "I was born in the '60s, during the time of real change." I lived in Munich, Germany, Texas, Florida, Maryland, New York, and North Carolina. I was an only child raised as the son of a US Army soldier who served two tours in Vietnam. Most of my travels were related to my father's career in the military. Both my parents came from Polish-born parents, so I was raised Catholic. I have an uncle who survived being in a concentration camp from World War II while my dad's sister was separated as a child from her parents and brother.

My mom was always a little eccentric over the years when I was growing up. Later, she was diagnosed with bipolar disorder. My work history in the service industry includes restaurants, sales, ten years at Goodwill Industries, ten years at a university in North Carolina.

I had a couple of businesses that I attempted to make work. One business was online embroidery and clothing sales, which was many years ago and before Facebook. The other business was retail sales of southwest-style furniture and accessories. They later failed in 2008 during the housing and financial crisis.

I started writing a rough draft of my book Middle-Class Jobs. At the time, it was far different from the current version and was labeled with a very long title. It took five weeks to write, another five weeks to print fifty copies at the printshop. In 2009, I sent the rough drafts to the people in congress and to the vice president's wife at the time, Jill Biden. The only response I got was a Christmas card from the vice presidential mansion every year.

In 2020, I decided to rewrite the rough draft. Rough is an understatement. I had to essentially rewrite the book and change some figures that were twelve years out-of-date. I was happy to find Fulton Books to publish my book, Middle-Class Jobs.

Besides life experiences, what do I know about policies and job creation? Goodwill Industries in Florida was probably one of the best feel-good jobs because of the number of jobs that were created in such a short time frame. The planning and strategies that I suggested throughout my ten years along with other coworkers and staff doubled the size of the whole operation in our region. I did go to college and studied statistics, microeconomics, politics, public speaking, business writing, and had a good relationship with my teachers and professors. SNL made fun of no one watching C-SPAN anyway. Guess what? I have watched C-SPAN for decades, PBS NewsHour, political shows on Sundays, documentaries, movies. I used to read about the Iraq-Iran War on page 30-something in the Miami Herald back in the '80s. I have studied charts, graphs, and votes of what little has become law as well as the national elections since 1980. I talk politics every day because everything is connected to politics. I have been a campaign worker for two national campaigns and one local race. I have voted my entire voting life and have donated to some campaigns. Lastly, I have read many books on politics, economics, history, biographies, and some fictitious books about possible outcomes of social, economic, and political systems. My hobbies include chess, World Domination video games, petting cats, analyzing stocks, analyzing elections, reading, writing, watching General Hospital, and most importantly, I like to talk.

Thank you for your interest, and I hope to continue writing books for the duration of my time on planet earth.